RACCOONS

For David

RACCOONS

By Bernice Kohn

Pictures by John Hamberger

Prentice-Hall, Inc., Englewood Cliffs, N.J.

RACCOONS by Bernice Kohn, pictures by John Hamberger
© 1968 by Bernice Kohn and John Hamberger
Library of Congress Catalog Card Number: 6 8 - 1 4 5 4 8
Printed in the United States of America   J
ISBN 0-13-749903-5

A raccoon always looks as if it is
    wearing a Halloween mask.
Behind the mask, shine two
    black, beady eyes. They are
    mischievous and ready for
    fun.
But a black line that runs from
    its forehead to its nose makes
    the raccoon look slightly
    worried, too.

Its ears are broad triangles and
are very alert.

The raccoon's scientific name is *Procyon*.
It belongs to the same family of mammals as the panda.
   Some other members of the family are the cacomistle,

the coati

and the kinkajou.

A full-grown raccoon is about the
    size of a small cocker spaniel.
It is covered with two kinds of
    hair.
There is an undercoat that is
    fine, short, and gray.
The top hair is grayish, too, but
    it is blackened at the tips. It is
    so long that it almost drags
    on the ground.
The beautiful, bushy tail is
    ringed with gray and black.
It is often ten inches long.

Even bigger than a raccoon's
    tail is its appetite.
Raccoons eat almost anything.
    They like berries, insects,
    mice, birds and frogs.
They even like soda and can
    quickly learn to drink from
    a bottle!

Because of their fondness for corn and other crops,
raccoons are often chased by farmers with their
coon dogs.

Before a raccoon eats anything, he likes to wash it in
water.

He holds the food in his forepaws and dips it up and
down, over and over again. He often continues long
after the food seems to be quite clean.

When the food is washed, the raccoon holds it in his
paws and tears off bites with his teeth.

A raccoon's teeth are much like a cat's. The front
teeth are long and sharp and the back ones are
wedge-shaped and good for grinding.

As soon as he has finished his
meal, the raccoon carefully
washes his paws.

Then he goes to sleep in the fork
of a tree.
He tucks his nose between his
toes and curls up until he
looks like a big, fat ball of fur.
With his black and gray color,
a raccoon is almost invisible
in the lights and shadows of
the tree.

He sleeps most of the day and
gets up at night to hunt for
food.
His home is always near water
and he is an excellent
swimmer.
To catch his food, he reaches his
slender fingers into the water
and pulls out salamanders,
fish, and mussels.

But when fall comes, the raccoon's habits change.
He has eaten well all summer and has put on enough
    fat to last him through the winter.
Now he crawls into his nest in a hollow tree and goes
    to sleep.

He doesn't wake up until the
    spring thaws come. Then he
    crawls out of his nest.
He is thin and weak and nearly
    starved.
He begins to search for food at
    once.

During April and May, the young are born.
There are usually three to six in a litter.
They are very small and helpless, and they are totally
blind for the first three weeks.

The babies don't leave the nest for two months, and the
mother tends them very carefully.
She nurses them with her milk until they are old
enough to eat solid food.

The babies have fluffy coats and the same markings
as the adults.
They all have black masks and ringed tails.

As soon as the youngsters are two months old, the
   mother takes them on their first trip through the
   forest.
The babies follow in single file.
Often, they lag behind to investigate things, then have
   to run to catch up.

If one of the babies gets lost, it cries in a high, sad wail,
   and the mother goes to search for it.

When there is any danger, the mother immediately
    shoves her family up a tree. Then she leads the
    enemy a mad chase through mud, marsh, and
    swamp.
If cornered, she fights furiously.
When she is certain that the danger is past, she
    returns to her babies.

Young raccoons remain with their mothers for a year.
At the end of that time, they are fully grown and
    ready to set out on their own.
They live for about ten years.

If you are in the country, listen
　　for the cry of a raccoon.
The sound that the adult makes
　　is very different from the
　　baby's cry.
It is harsh, loud, and has a bit of
　　a whistle in it.
You might mistake it for the call
　　of a screech owl.

On a spring day, when the ground is soft, look for
raccoon tracks near a stream.
Each track is about two inches long and shows a heel
and five toes.
The tracks may be from one-half inch to more than a
foot apart, depending on how fast the raccoon
was traveling.

Young raccoons make delightful pets.
They are friendly and affectionate — and very, very
  curious.
They explore everything, and even learn how to open
  closets and bureau drawers.

They are especially clever about
    getting into the kitchen
    cupboards.
If you keep a pet raccoon, watch
    out! All of your sweets might
    disappear.
And so might your jewelry or
    anything else that glitters.
Raccoons love to play with shiny
    objects.

When you see a raccoon in the woods or in a zoo,
attract its attention with a shiny coin or a ring.
The raccoon won't be able to resist.

You will suddenly have a new friend!